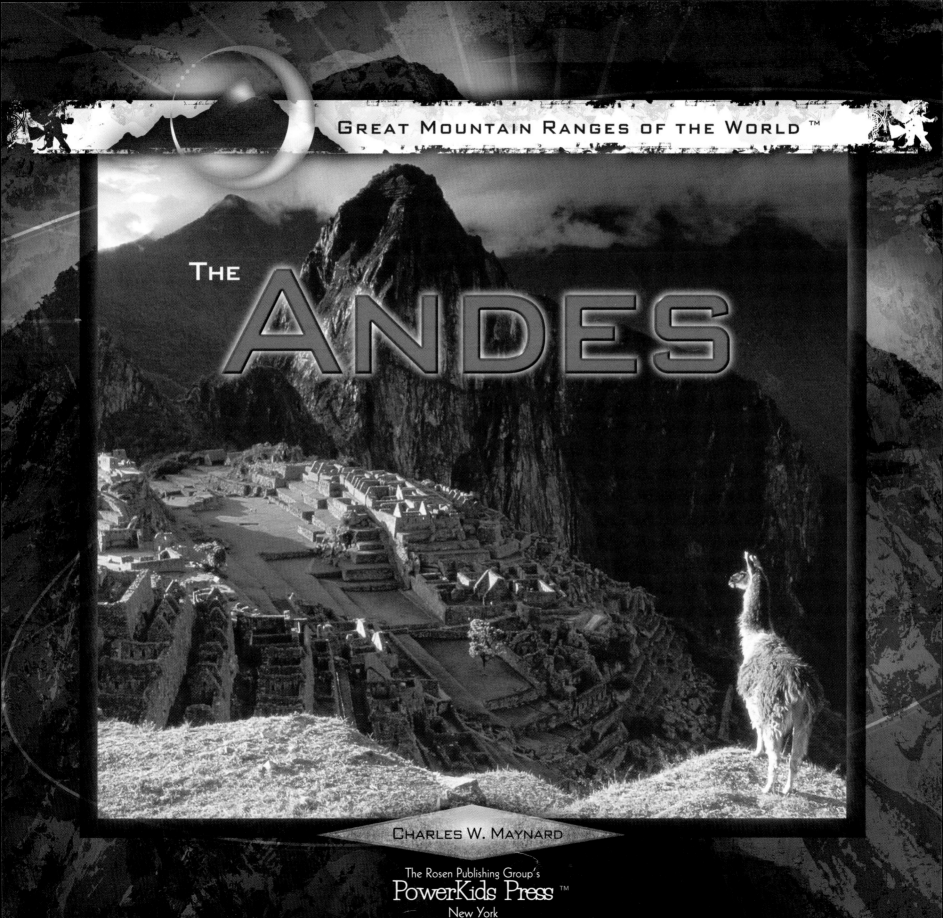

THE ANDES

CHARLES W. MAYNARD

The Rosen Publishing Group's
PowerKids Press ™
New York

For John and Lou, my parents, who explored the Bolivian Andes with me firsthand, and to the next generations, Doug, Kelsie, Lucy, Courtney, Drew, Kelly, Laura, Dawson, Danielle, Kaylee, and Caleb, who will explore other mountains.

Published in 2004 by The Rosen Publishing Group, Inc.
29 East 21st Street, New York, NY 10010

First Edition

Editor: Frances E. Ruffin
Book Design: Emily Muschinske
Photo Researcher: Barbara Koppelman

Photo Credits: Cover and pp. 1, 11 © Frans Lanting/Minden Pictures; pp. 4, 7 © Galen Rowell/CORBIS; p. 7 (bottom) © U.S. Geological Survey/Science Photo Library/Photo Researchers; p. 8 © George F. Mobley/National Geographic Image Collection; p. 8 (inset) © Layne Kennedy/CORBIS; p. 11 (inset) © Peter Oxford/Nature Picture Library; p. 12 © Pablo Corral Vega/CORBIS; p. 12 (inset left) © Wolfgang Kaehler; p. 12 (inset bottom) © François Gohier/Photo Researchers; p. 15 © Brigit Koch/Animals Animals; p. 15 (inset) Tui De Roy/Minden Pictures; p. 16 © Sergio Pitamitz/CORBIS; p. 19 © Getty Images; p. 19 (inset) © Craig Lovell/CORBIS; p. 20 © Hideo Haga/HAGA/The Image Works.

002013501

Manufactured in the United States of America

CONTENTS

PANAMA
VENEZUELA
GEORGETOWN
PARAMARIBO
CAYENNE
FRENCH
GUIANA
Caribbean
Sea
COLOMBIA
BOGOTÁ
ECUADOR
QUITO
The Amazon River
BRAZIL
PERU
LIMA
BOLIVIA
LA PAZ
BRASÍLIA
Pacific
Ocean
SUCRE
PARAGUAY
ASUNCIÓN
URUGUAY
SANTIAGO
BUENOS
AIRES
MONTEVIDEO
ARGENTINA
Atlantic
Ocean
ANDES
ANDES
CHILE

SOUTH AMERICA

MILES OF MOUNTAINS

South America's Andes mountain range is the longest in the world. It begins in the north in Colombia and Venezuela and stretches about 5,000 miles (8,047 km) south through seven countries. The mountains end at the tip of South America at Tierra del Fuego, Argentina. The Andes run **parallel** to South America's west coast and the Pacific Ocean. The Andes tower over broad plains that stretch eastward from the mountains to the Atlantic coast. Mount Aconcagua, at more than 22,800 feet (6,949 m), is the highest peak in the Andes, as well as the highest peak in the **Western Hemisphere**. Aconcagua, which rises to more than 4 miles (6 km) above **sea level** in Argentina, is near the border of Chile. The Andes are rich in copper, tin, gold, silver, lead, mercury, and sulfur. Early people who lived there more than 1,000 years ago mined gold and silver. They used the metals to make beautiful objects, which they used in worship or buried with their dead. In the 1500s and 1600s, Spanish explorers searched the Andes for gold and other **minerals**, which they sent back to Spain.

These jagged peaks of the Andes in Patagonia seem to pierce the clouds. Incan people who lived in the Andes called their land the land of four corners, or suyus. One suyu was named Antisuyu. Spanish explorers named the mountains the Andes for the Incan name Anti.

RING OF FIRE

The Andes are part of the **geological** Ring of Fire that circles the Pacific Ocean. The Ring of Fire is a ring of active volcanoes that borders the great **continental plates** of the Pacific Ocean. There are more active volcanoes in the Ring of Fire than in any other place on Earth. Volcanoes occur all around the Pacific Ocean. The Pacific plates frequently collide with plates of the continents that border the ocean. When this occurs, they create a **subduction zone**, in which one of the plates is pushed below another. This causes the two plates to grind together. The **friction** between the plates, combined with the heat from Earth's **core**, melts rock into **magma**, a hot sticky rock. The magma is powerfully forced to Earth's surface. As the magma cools, it can begin to form a volcano. Constant movement of the South American and the Pacific plates has created more than 50 active volcanoes in the Andes.

MOUNTAINS FACT

THE WORLD'S HIGHEST ACTIVE VOLCANO LIES IN ECUADOR NEAR THE EQUATOR. THIS VOLCANO, COTOPAXI, IS 19,347 FEET (5,897 M) HIGH. IN 1744, AN ERUPTION OF COTOPAXI WAS HEARD MORE THAN 500 MILES (805 KM) AWAY.

This crater (above) is in the Cotopaxi volcano in Ecuador.

Inset: This satellite shows locations of volcanoes around the Ring of Fire. Based on sea level, the scale at the far right measures the height of mountains and the depth of the ocean.

ASIA

NORTH AMERICA

PACIFIC OCEAN

SOUTH AMERICA

NEW ZEALAND

Meters

SEA LEVEL

+5000

+3500

+2000

+1000

0

-1500

-3000

-5000

-7000

-9000

RISING MOUNTAINS

The Andes were created from 20 to 25 million years ago, when the South American and the Pacific plates bumped together. In the northern Andes, the mountains have "wrinkled" into three ranges called cordilleras. Cordilleras are chains of mountains that run parallel to each other. Flat **plateaus** between the cordilleras are called **altiplanos**. Lake Titicaca lies in the altiplano of Bolivia and Peru. This large, high-**altitude**, freshwater lake is what is left of a much larger lake that formed millions of years ago as the cordilleras rose on both sides of it.

Though many mountains continue to rise slowly, **glaciers** of ice and snow on the mountains are also slowly wearing them down. Melting snow and ice form rivers. The rivers that flow west from the Andes to the Pacific Ocean, such as the Santa River of Peru, are short and narrow. Those that flow east toward the Atlantic Ocean, such as the Amazon River, are long and have a lot of water. The Amazon River begins its journey high in the Andes. At 4,000 miles (6,437 km) long it is the second-longest river in the world.

Glaciers are formed on peaks such as these in the Cordillera de Paine in Chile. These glaciers melt and become rivers, such as the Tigre River (inset), which flows through a Peruvian rain forest. The Tigre River flows east and becomes part of the great Amazon River.

A Range of Weather

Climates in the Andes, like those in any other mountain range, depend upon **elevation** and **latitude**. The Andes run south through seven countries, from north of the **equator** in Venezuela to Argentina's Tierra del Fuego, near Antarctica. This makes Andean climates vary greatly. Climates also change from warm and humid **tropical** regions at sea level to very cold and snowy areas in the high altitudes of the mountain peaks.

On the eastern side of the Andes, in smaller hills, lie tropical **rain forests**. South America's hot, humid rain forests can have more than 100 inches (254 cm) of rain per year. Deserts lie between the Andes and the Pacific Ocean. The altiplanos, at 11,500 to 13,000 feet (3,505–3,962 m), are cool and dry with few trees. Strong winds stir up great clouds of dust. High peaks above the altiplanos are covered with snow and ice year-round.

MOUNTAIN FACT

IN CHILE, THE SOUTHERN RANGES OF THE ANDES HAVE A CLIMATE SIMILAR TO THAT OF THE CONTINENT OF ANTARCTICA. ON THE HIGHEST PEAKS, THE AIR IS THIN, WITH LESS THAN ONE-HALF OF THE OXYGEN THAT THERE IS AT SEA LEVEL.

This is a palm swamp in Peru. Inset: *The Valley of the Moon in Chile's Atacama Desert seems like a place out of this world.*

PLANT LIFE

A variety of plants grows in the many climates of the Andes. Trees and flowers are plentiful in the rain forests. Ferns, orchids, and mahogany trees are only a few of the many plant and tree **species** that live there.

The altiplanos appear to have few plants and even fewer trees. However, eucalyptus trees have been introduced there and grow around houses and villages. Animals such as the llama and the alpaca feed on ichu grass, which grows on the altiplanos. People use ichu grass to make roofs for their houses. Totora reeds grow thickly along the shores of Lake Titicaca. People have used these reeds for centuries to make boats to travel the blue waters of this high lake. The potato was first grown in the Andes and later was introduced to the world by Spaniards who visited the mountains during the 1500s. The Andes regions are famous for the coca plant, used by Andean people for hundreds of years. Today modern medicines are made from the coca plant.

Workers in a potato field harvest potatoes in San Isidro, Venezuela. Left Inset: A man and a child make a boat using totora reeds at Lake Titicaca, Peru. Right Inset: A pink orchid grows in an Amazon rain forest.

High-Altitude Animals

Many interesting animals make their homes in the Andes. One amazing creature is the Andean condor, the largest flying bird on Earth. These huge birds have wingspans of more than 10 feet (3 m). They can fly more than 20,000 feet (6,096 m) above sea level. These large birds have became rare because some people hunt them for sport. Another rare animal is the ucumari, or spectacled bear, which is black except for white rings around its eyes. Perhaps one of the most famous Andean animals is the long-necked llama, a member of the camel family. It has many relatives in the Andes. The vicuña, the smallest llama relative, lives in the cold climates of the high Andes. Vicuñas are wild and are becoming very rare. Another cousin, the guanaco, lives in the mountains and in the coastal plains. The alpaca, like the llama, is domesticated. It is raised as a farm animal.

MOUNTAIN FACT

LLAMAS HAVE CARRIED THE BURDENS OF ANDEAN PEOPLE THROUGH THE MOUNTAINS FOR HUNDREDS OF YEARS. LLAMAS ARE ALSO A SOURCE OF MEAT. THEY AND ALPACAS ARE RAISED FOR THEIR WOOL. WARM CLOTHING THAT KEEPS OUT THE ANDEAN CHILL IS MADE FROM THE WOOL OF ALPACAS AND LLAMAS.

This llama cannot really read signs. It resembles its cousin the camel. Inset: The Andean condor is the world's largest flying bird.

CHIAPA 20
JAIÑA 30
COLCHANE

PEOPLE OF THE ANDES

The Andes wind through Venezuela, Colombia, Ecuador, Peru, Bolivia, Chile, and Argentina. Few people live in the Andes mountains of Chile and Argentina because of the severe winters in these regions. Millions of people live in the mountains and the altiplanos of the other countries, as farmers and as herders of livestock. However, farming can be difficult on the Andean high plateaus. The growing season is short. Many people earn a living by mining some of the rich mineral resources of the mountains.

Several cities in the high mountains have large populations. La Paz, Bolivia, with more than 700,000 people, is the world's highest capital city, at around 12,000 feet (3,658 m).

Spanish is the main language spoken throughout the Andes. Aymara, a native language, is also spoken in many areas, as is Quechua, the language of the Inca. In fact, Bolivia uses all three as national languages. Andean music is known for its use of drums, pipes, and flutes that are made of reeds.

The lovely sounds of Andean music are made by the panpipes, the reed instrument that this man in Purmamarca, Argentina, is playing.

EARLY PEOPLES

People settled in the Andes more than 10,000 years ago. Almost 3,000 years ago, some Andean people lived in small towns and grew their food on farms outside of the towns. The Tiwanaka, a civilized **culture**, lived on the shores of Lake Titicaca from A.D. 500 to 1000. The Tiwanakans farmed the altiplanos of present-day Bolivia and Peru to support their cities.

The Nazca people lived along the Pacific coast of Peru around the same time. They drew pictures on the desert floor that were hundreds of feet (m) long, showing insects, animals, and other objects. The Aymara people built hill towns on the altiplanos, but were conquered by the Incas in the 1400s. In the 1500s, the Spanish conquered the Incas and gained control of the Andes and South America. By the 1800s, Spanish control was overthrown and many of the present-day countries were formed.

MOUNTAIN FACT

THE INCAS RULED AN EMPIRE THAT HAD MORE THAN 12 MILLION PEOPLE, AND THAT STRETCHED NEARLY 2,500 MILES (4,023 KM). ALMOST 10,000 MILES (16,093 KM) OF ROADS LINKED THE EMPIRE. THE INCAS PAVED THEIR ROADS WITH LARGE, FLAT STONES. THEY BUILT ROADS THROUGH JUNGLES, AND OVER MOUNTAINS AND ALTIPLANOS.

Huge birds and other shapes drawn by the Nazca people still exist on the Plains of Nazca. Inset: This ruin in Bolivia was a temple to the Sun.

Incan Legends

The Incas had an advanced culture in many ways, yet they had no written language or system of numbers. They used quipus, a series of knotted cords and strings, to keep their records. Valuable information about how the Incas lived was stored in the quipus through the different colors of yarn, knots, and turns within the knots. People who were trained to be quipu "rememberers" understood the knots.

The Incas believed that the creator of Earth was called Viracocha, and that he first made people on the southern shores of Lake Titicaca. Appearing as an old white man with a walking stick, Viracocha walked to the north and then across the Pacific. The Incas believed that Viracocha would return in times of trouble.

Gold and silver were important to the Incas, who used them for offerings to the gods and for decorations. They said that gold was "the sweat of the sun," and that silver was "the tears of the moon."

This photograph shows the colorful and exciting Cuzco Inca Festival in Cuzco, Peru. The event observes the coming of winter.

THE LOST CITY

In 1911, Hiram Bingham of Yale University, in Connecticut, found Machu Picchu, an ancient Incan city high in the Andes. Today it is known as the Lost City of the Incas, and it is one of the most-visited ruins in the Andes. Many people disagree about the original purpose of this interesting city. It might have been a city, or it might have been either a fort protecting the city of Cuzco or a temple to the Sun. Machu Picchu's stonework and its 3,000 steplike terraces of land are amazing examples of how the Incan people carved places to live in the steep Andes mountains.

Scientists continue to learn more about the Incas and other peoples who lived in the Andes many years ago. In 1995, one **expedition** found the **mummy** of a young girl frozen in the ice high on Mount Ampato in Peru. People called her the Ice Maiden. In 1998, other explorers found three mummies on Cerro Llullaillaco at more than 22,000 feet (6,706 m). This discovery is the world's highest **archaeological** site. It is believed that the Incas sacrificed people to their gods. These mummies have provided many clues as to how the Incan people lived and what they believed.

GLOSSARY

altiplanos (al-ti-PLAH-nohs) A Spanish word for high plains.

altitude (AL-tih-tood) The height above Earth's surface.

archaeological (ar-kee-uh-LAH-jih-kul) Having to do with the way humans lived a long time ago.

climates (KLY-mits) The kind of weather certain areas have.

continental plates (kon-tin-EN-tul PLAYTS) The moving pieces of Earth's crust.

core (KOR) The hot center of Earth that is made of liquid rock.

culture (KUL-chur) The beliefs, practices, art, and religions of a group of people.

elevation (eh-luh-VAY-shun) The height of an object.

equator (ih-KWAY-tur) An imaginary line around Earth that separates it into two parts, northern and southern.

expedition (ek-spuh-DIH-shun) A trip for a special purpose.

friction (FRIK-shin) The rubbing of one thing against another.

geological (jee-uh-LAH-jih-kul) Relating to Earth's rocks and minerals.

glaciers (GLAY-shurz) Large masses of ice that move down a mountain or along a valley.

latitude (LA-tih-tood) The distance north or south of the equator, measured by degrees.

magma (MAG-muh) A hot, liquid rock underneath Earth's surface.

minerals (MIH-ner-ulz) Natural elements that are not animals, plants or other living things.

mummy (MUH-mee) In most instances, a body that had been prepared for burial in a way that makes it last a long time.

parallel (PAR-uh-lel) Facing the same direction as another object.

plateaus (pla-TOHZ) Broad, flat, high pieces of land.

rain forests (RAYN FOR-ests) Thick forests that receive large amounts of rain.

sea level (SEE LEH-vul) The height of the top of the ocean.

species (SPEE-sheez) A single kind of plant or animal. All people are one species.

subduction zone (sub-DUK-shun ZOHN) The place where a crack forms when two plates hit and one forces the other into Earth's mantle.

tropical (TRAH-puh-kul) Having to do with the warm areas of Earth that are near the equator.

Western Hemisphere (WES-tern HEH-muh-sfeer) The western half of Earth.

INDEX

WEB SITES

Due to the changing nature of Internet links, Powerkids Press has developed an online list of Web sites related to the subject of this book. This site is upgraded regularly. Please use this link to access the list:

www.powerkidslinks.com/gmrw/andes